M000098192

Wing It!

FLAVORFUL
CHICKEN WINGS,
SAUCES AND
SIDES

ROBERT QUINTANA

PHOTOGRAPHY BY
JON EDWARDS

GIBBS SMITH
TO ENRICH AND INSPIRE HUMANKIND

I would like to dedicate this book to Shelley, my wife;
thank you for closing all those kitchen cabinet doors I've left open.

I would like to acknowledge Mark Miller; his zest for life and knowledge is unrivaled.
He has mentored and exposed me to all his experiences. Thanks for including me in your journey.

First Edition
17 16 15 14 13   5 4 3 2 1

Text © 2013 by Robert Quintana
Photographs © 2013 by Jon Edwards
Photo assistant: Heather Winters

All rights reserved. No part of this book may be reproduced by any means whatsoever without
written permission from the publisher, except brief portions quoted for purpose of review.

Published by
Gibbs Smith
P.O. Box 667
Layton, Utah 84041

1.800.835.4993 orders
www.gibbs-smith.com

Designed by Michelle Farinella Design

Gibbs Smith books are printed on paper produced from sustainable
PEFC-certified forest/controlled wood source. Learn more at www.pefc.org.
Printed and bound in Hong Kong

Library of Congress Cataloging-in-Publication Data

Quintana, Robert.
Wing it! : flavorful chicken wings, sauces and sides / Robert Quintana ;
photographs by Jon Edwards. -- First edition.
pages cm
Includes index.
ISBN 978-1-4236-3386-0
1. Cooking (Chicken) I. Title.
TX750.5.C45Q58 2013
641.6'65--dc23
2012051240

Contents

Preface

What is it about eating chicken wings that gets people all excited? Over the last decade the popularity of wings has soared. When I roast a chicken, the first part I love to eat are the wings. The use of chicken wings and drumettes has gained a huge following by both young and old and on restaurant menus. The reasons are simple; chicken is what I refer to as the "empty canvas." The range of recipes can satisfy most every palate; from local flavors like smoke and barbecue, to more exotic international spices like curry and Moroccan *ras el hanout*. Everyone has a favorite flavor and looks for a new version to excite the daily routine or impress partygoers. This is where the experimentation and personal preferences come into play. Taking the ordinary and making it extraordinary! Layering flavor as one would paint.

My chicken wing focus starts with basic fresh chicken whose flavors can many times be easily enhanced by layering in marinades or brines. Today's choices of free-range and organic chickens are plentiful, so look for the best and start to create family traditions. The savory recipes in this book are only a starting point and are enhanced by one's imagination.

These recipes are great for all types of family and friend parties and gatherings. Creating your own sauces may seem difficult when compared to opening a bottle, but it is worth experiencing the flavors, and the education obtained is unforgettable. One of the best aspects of cooking wings is that you really can't go wrong with the cooking process.

My ideas for this book come from personal experience as an international traveler and lover of imaginative cookery. As a lifelong chef, I have had the privilege of cooking and tasting wonderful foods from all over the world. I hope this compilation of aromas, tastes, and ideas is as enjoyable to you as it has been for me.

Wing it, enjoy!

Robert Quintana
Santa Fe and Los Angeles

CHICKEN QUALITY

Natural

A chicken that contains no artificial ingredients or added color and is only minimally processed is considered to be natural. Minimal processing means the chicken was processed in a manner that doesn't fundamentally alter the product. The label must explain the meaning of natural, such as no artificial ingredients, or if it contains water.

Free-Range

Chickens that are free-range have access to fenced yards where the birds roam in open air and forage through the native grass pastures, are not fed on organic feeds, and are given a vegetarian diet of corn and soybeans. They are not given antibiotics.

Organic Certified

The USDA must certify organic feeds and everything that goes into the chicken must be certified as well. The lists of ingredients that are not allowed include animal by-products, genetically modified organisms (GMOs), antibiotics, pesticide-treated grains, grains grown with chemical fertilizers, and synthetic amino acids. Chickens are fed a basic diet of organic corn, organic soybeans, organic wheat, vitamins, and minerals. They also feed on grass and insects from the pasture they are grown in.

Air Chilling Verses Conventional Water Chilled

Air chilling is better for the flavor of chicken; it also inhibits the spread of bacteria by keeping the chickens independent. With water chilling, the chickens are commingled in chlorinated cold water that absorbs into the meat, affecting its flavor.

Bird Age and Sizes

Most birds develop in about 9 weeks. Average weights vary from 4–6 pounds and are categorized as poussin roasters, fryers, and capons.

Recommended Brands

> Mary's Chickens, free range, air chilled
> Bell & Evans Air-Chilled Chicken
> Rosie Organic, Petaluma Poultry
> Rocky Jr. Free-Range Chicken, Petaluma Poultry
> Springer Mountain Farms, fresh chicken
> Empire Kosher, water cooled and koshered (salted and soaked)

ROASTING AND BLACKENING TOMATOES

Roasting and blackening tomatoes gives them a more rustic, robust, and complex flavor. It concentrates the sugars and reduces water content. Also, roasting and blackening helps in the preservation of a sauce if the sauce is not consumed all in one day. Smaller tomatoes have a more concentrated umami flavor and are found year round. When choosing tomatoes, look for uniform size, darkest color possible on the vine, and consider heirloom and local varieties.

Roasting

Place tomatoes in a heavy-bottom cast iron pan or comal, heated to medium low, turning often and not blackening, about 8 minutes total for cherry tomatoes, 10–12 minutes total for Early Girls, 12–14 minutes total for Roma tomatoes, and 14–16 minutes for larger varieties. This can also be done in the oven with a broiler set to 425 degrees, rack centered in oven, for the same approximate times.

Blackening

Place tomatoes in a heavy-bottom cast iron pan or comal, heated to medium high, let set for 4 minutes making sure to blacken the skin well, turn over and blacken the other side for 4 more minutes for cherry tomatoes, 8–10 minutes total for Early Girls, 10–12 minutes total for Roma tomatoes, and larger varieties for 12–14 minutes total.

Fire Roasting

Place tomatoes on a grill grate set over an open flame on medium heat, turning every minute or until the skin blisters, being careful not to fully burn. Do not over blacken or a bitter taste will result. A hand-held butane torch can also be used.

Oven Dried

Preheat oven to 225 degrees. Prepare a large pot of boiling water. Prepare a large ice bath. Score the bottom of Roma tomatoes and core; plunge in boiling water for 10–15 seconds, remove and place in the ice water. Peel the skin and cut the Roma tomatoes lengthwise in half, place in a bowl, and season with salt and desired flavorings such as garlic, herbs, spices, and chile powders. Place cut side down on a baking sheet and dry in oven for 2 hours. If not using immediately, tomatoes can be stored in a jar covered with olive oil.

ROASTING FRESH CHILES AND BELL PEPPERS

Roasting chiles and bell peppers brings out the natural sweetness, enhances their complex flavors, and adds a robust smokey element. This technique also helps in peeling the tough skin, which can be bitter. When it is important to retain the color and not need the element of smoke in chiles or bell peppers, oil roasting is preferable. After you have handled chiles, do not touch your face or eyes until you have washed your hands thoroughly. Wearing rubber gloves is recommended. The work area in which you have placed the chiles needs to be thoroughly cleaned.

Fire Roasting

Place the chiles or bell peppers over an open flame covered with a grill grate, on a barbecue grill, or under a broiler; a hand-held butane torch can also be used. Blister and blacken the skins all over, being careful not to burn the flesh. Transfer to a bowl and cover with plastic wrap, or place in a ziplock bag and let steam for 15–20 minutes. Remove the skins with your fingers or with the tip of a small knife. Remove the seeds and ribs if the recipe calls for it. Removing the seeds and ribs will diminish the heat of the chiles. Never wash the chiles under water, as this will remove the natural oils and the capsicum.

Oil Roasting

In a large, deep frying pan, heat 1 cup canola oil to 350 degrees. Place the chiles or bell peppers in the pan and blister the skin for 1 minute on each side until all the skin has blistered; use caution as the oil and water from the chiles will splatter. The use of a frying screen is recommended. Place the chiles or bell peppers in a bowl and cover with plastic wrap, or place in a ziplock bag and let steam for 15– 20 minutes. Remove the skins with your fingers or with the tip of a small knife. Remove the seeds and ribs if the recipe calls for it.

Dry Roasting

Place chiles in a heavy-bottom cast iron pan, heated to medium, and roast for 8–12 minutes depending on the size. This method works well for smaller chiles and jalapeño peppers with thinner skins.

ROASTING GARLIC

Dry Roasting

Place unpeeled garlic cloves in a heavy-bottom cast iron pan and dry roast the garlic over medium-low heat for 15–20 minutes, turning occasionally until the garlic softens and browns on the outside. When roasted, you should be able to squeeze the garlic out of the clove. Roasted garlic is smokey and mellow and sweeter and subtler in flavor than raw garlic. Raw garlic flavors can dominate other ingredients and over a small period of time will take over a whole dish. Blanching garlic in boiling salted water is recommended if you want a less aggressive garlic flavor.

Oven Roasted

Preheat oven to 350 degrees. Place the garlic in a heavy-bottom frying pan and bake uncovered for 40 minutes.

Oil Roasted

Preheat oven to 350 degrees. In a small, oven-safe frying pan with a lid, add ¾ cup canola or olive oil and peeled, whole garlic cloves (about 20); season with salt. Bake, covered, for 30–40 minutes. If desired, herbs can be added to flavor the oil.

Smoked Garlic

To smoke garlic in a stovetop smoker, fill the bottom with apple wood chips, cover with second internal pan and wire rack set on top of that pan. Cut the top off the whole garlic bulb, just enough to expose the inside, cutting ⅛ inch into the garlic cloves. Place the garlic in the smoker and put on the stove. Heat the gas flame to high and ignite the wood chips for 2–3 minutes; turn to low to keep the smoke going and continue for 20 minutes more. Place the smoker in a preheated oven set to 400 degrees and cook an additional 20 minutes.

ROASTING ONIONS AND SHALLOTS

Whole Roasted Onions

Preheat oven to 450 degrees. Place medium, whole, sweet variety onions with the root side up in a large heavy-bottom frying pan lined with parchment paper (this will help in the clean up) and bake for 2 hours. The outside onion skin will burn but let the onions cook the full 2 hours and then cool completely. Peel away the skin and use the inner parts. These onions get better with time when left to absorb the sweeter roasted outer layer.

Blackened Onions

Preheat a heavy-bottom cast iron pan on medium low. Slice onions into ⅓-inch rings and place directly on the pan. Let the onions crust for about 6 minutes, flip over and roast the other side for an additional 6 minutes. The volume loss is about half so it is helpful to roast extra onions.

Roasting Shallots

Preheat oven to 350 degrees. Peel shallots, cut in half, and season with salt. Lightly oil a baking sheet and lay shallots cut side down. Bake for 35–40 minutes.

Fried Shallots

In a large sauté pan, preheat ⅓ cup of peanut oil to 350 degrees. Slice 1½ cups shallots, lengthwise in thin julienne strips, and sauté for about 4–5 minutes turning often until golden brown. Remove to a paper towel. Makes ¾ cup.

TOASTING AND HYDRATING DRIED CHILES AND SEEDS

Toasting dried chiles activates the oils in the skins, giving added flavor. The seeds can also be toasted to add a nuttiness, heat, and a smokey element to certain salsas.

Preheat a cast iron pan to low heat or preheat oven to 250 degrees. Stem and remove as many seeds as possible, add the seeds to the pan, and shake continuously for about 1½ minutes, or double the time if cooking in an oven. The seeds will continue to cook so it is important to remove them from the hot pan and transfer to a plate. Use a spice mill to grind seeds.

Toast chiles by placing in a single layer in a cast iron pan and toast for 2 minutes on each side, making sure not to over toast or a bitter taste may result. Remove and place in a bowl with enough hot water

to cover and place a plate on top to keep the chiles submerged under water for 20 minutes to rehydrate them.

Taste the water to see if it has a bitter taste, if so, drain the chiles and use new water or some portion of the hydrating liquid if you will be using the chiles in a sauce.

TOASTING DRIED SPICES, HERBS, AND SEEDS

Toasting enhances and intensifies flavors of dried spices, herbs, and seeds. Toasting activates the essential oils and brings out the fragrance, which helps in flavor recognition.

Place a nonstick sauté pan over low heat and toast herbs and spices, such as oregano, coriander, or cumin for 1–2 minutes or until fragrant, stirring frequently. Use caution as these dried ingredients can scorch easily, causing bitterness. The use of whole spices that are toasted and freshly ground are recommended, as pre ground spices lose their aromatic quality and are not as flavorful.

Toasting Sesame Seeds

In a Japanese sesame seed roaster, or in a small wire basket over a low, open flame, toast sesame seeds for 1 minute, stirring constantly.

HEAT LEVELS AND COUNTRY

The heat levels listed for each recipe are on a scale of 1 to 10 with 1 being very mild and 10 being very, very hot. If you are not used to eating spicy foods, prepare each dish to your liking when using chiles and spices. You can eliminate the seeds in the chiles or use only a small amount since that is where the heat is most concentrated.

I have included the country or state where these recipes are based, for inspiration and a guideline of traditional flavors and techniques used in these regions.

Chinese Tea-Smoked Wings

Tea is the quintessential Chinese beverage and is the second most popular drink in the world after water. It not only cleanses the palate, it also facilitates the blending of flavors, which is what makes this recipe work so well. Tea is becoming so popular, in fact, that mixologists (or bartenders, as they were once called) make up delectable concoctions using tea-infused liquors. So, in keeping with that spirit, I've included a "MarTEAni" recipe to add to the festivities. Allow 24 hours preparation time.

3 cups brewed Lapsang Souchong tea

1 teaspoon salt

3 cloves garlic, crushed

2 tablespoons grated fresh ginger

3 green onions, chopped

2 tablespoons honey

2 tablespoons organic soy sauce

¼ cup light soy sauce

½ cup sherry

2 tablespoons black vinegar

1 teaspoon white pepper

2½ pounds chicken wings, cut at the joint and rinsed in cold water

1 cup jasmine rice

1 cup brown sugar

1 cup loose Lapsang Souchong tea leaves

In a large bowl, mix together the brewed tea, salt, garlic, ginger, onions, honey, soy sauce, light soy sauce, sherry, vinegar, and pepper. Add the chicken wings and marinate in the refrigerator for 24 hours.

Place the rice, brown sugar, and tea leaves in an even layer in the middle of a large, heavy-duty piece of aluminum foil and fold the foil into a flat square package. Line the bottom of a large, lidded wok with foil and place the tea package on top. Place a wire rack in the wok, and then place the wings on the rack, layering as evenly as possible. To smoke the wings, turn the heat on high and cover with a lid. As the smoke starts, reduce heat to medium and let cook for 30 minutes. Check the temperature of the chicken making sure an internal temperature of 165–170 degrees has been reached. Turn off heat and leave covered for 20 minutes more. Reheat just before serving with Sour Plum Jam.

continued

SOUR PLUM JAM

Makes 2⅓ cups

12 ounces fresh plums
1 cup sugar
¼ cup rice wine vinegar
3 Fresno chile peppers, seeds removed
   and minced
1 tablespoon ginger juice
3 tablespoons crystallized ginger
   (Reed's brand)

Remove pits from the plums and dice into ¼-inch pieces. Place in a medium saucepan with sugar, vinegar, peppers, and ginger juice. Simmer for 10 minutes, remove from heat, and fold in the crystallized ginger. Serve with wings as a dip.

MARTEANI

Makes 1 serving

3 ounces brewed jasmine tea, cooled
1½ ounces dark rum
3 drops Angostura Bitters
½ orange, juiced
4 ounces ice

Combine all ingredients in a cocktail shaker; shake and strain. Enjoy.

Indian Tandoori Chicken Drumettes

This Indian classic is traditionally cooked in a cone-shaped clay tandoor oven at an extremely high temperature, which produces a juicy and tender chicken. To reproduce the tandoor oven, preheat your oven to 500 degrees for 1 hour and then reduce the temperature to 450 degrees. The heat of the chile paste is mellowed by the yogurt marinade and the mango chutney. The famous red color comes from the sun-dried tomato paste and saffron, not food coloring which most restaurants use. This recipe also works well for chicken legs and thighs. Allow 3 hours preparation time.

WING MARINADE

2½ pounds chicken wing drumettes, rinsed
   in cold water
3 small dried ghost chiles or
   2 fresh habañero chiles
2 teaspoons salt
1 lemon, juiced
2 tablespoons sun-dried tomato concentrate
½ teaspoon ground saffron

Remove excess skin from drumettes and cut slits into the meat so the marinade can penetrate.

Use caution when working with ghost chiles; always wear gloves and never touch your eyes or any part of your body. Place the whole chiles in a spice mill and add the salt. Place a dry towel over the mill and grind the chiles; do not remove the lid for 5 minutes.

Carefully remove the lid of the spice mill and place the ground chiles and salt, lemon juice, tomato concentrate, and saffron in a large bowl and mix together to make a paste. Add the drumettes to the bowl making sure to get the paste in all the cut slits. Marinate for 20 minutes in the refrigerator.

continued

YOGURT MARINADE

1 cup whole milk yogurt
3 tablespoons minced garlic
1 tablespoon grated fresh ginger
2 teaspoons grated fresh turmeric or 1
  teaspoon dried
2 tablespoons grated white onion
4 teaspoons ground cumin, toasted
1 tablespoon garam masala
1½ teaspoons ground coriander, toasted
½ teaspoon ground fenugreek
1 teaspoon cayenne pepper
1½ teaspoons pepper
½ teaspoon ground green cardamom
1 teaspoon salt
1 tablespoon canola oil

Place the yogurt, garlic, ginger, turmeric, onion, cumin, garam masala, coriander, fenugreek, cayenne, pepper, cardamom, and salt into a large bowl and mix well. Transfer drumettes to the yogurt marinade; add the oil and mix to coat. Place in the refrigerator and marinate for 2 hours.

Preheat oven to 500 degrees for 1 hour and then reduce temperature to 450 degrees.

Lay the wings on a wire rack placed on a baking sheet that has been lined with foil. Bake for 25 minutes. Preheat grill to medium hot and finish the wings on the grill, making sure to char well. Serve with Fresh Pickled Mango Chutney.

FRESH PICKLED MANGO CHUTNEY

Makes 1½ cups

¼ cup white vinegar
1 mango, peeled, cut off the pit, and thinly sliced
1 tablespoon jaggery or brown sugar
½ teaspoon salt
¼ teaspoon ground fenugreek
⅛ teaspoon ground cardamom
¼ teaspoon ground coriander
¼ teaspoon ground grains of paradise
2 teaspoons New Mexico red chile flakes or cayenne pepper
Zest of 1 lime
1 tablespoon lime juice
1 teaspoon ginger juice

Place the vinegar and mango in a small bowl. Put the sugar and salt in a mortar then add the fenugreek, cardamom, coriander, grains of paradise, chile flakes, and lime zest; grind together. Add the spice mixture to vinegar and mango. Add lime juice and ginger juice and let marinate in refrigerator for 2 hours.

Lemongrass Mango Wings

Green curry is one of my favorite Thai flavors. It consists of fresh green Thai chiles, shallots, garlic, galangal, lemongrass, kaffir lime leaves, fresh coriander roots, and dried shrimp all ground to a paste in a mortar. (If you're adventurous and want to try to make your own, I have included a recipe, but the Mae Ploy brand is also a very good product.) Sprinkle the wings after they come off the grill with the Kaffir Lime Leaf Salt to enhance the jungle theme. The Lemongrass Mango Sauce is the perfect tropical complement to the richness of the curry. This recipe would also be great with grilled chicken breasts cut into strips. Allow 24 hours preparation time.

THAI GREEN CURRY BRINE

4 cups water

1 tablespoon salt

1 tablespoon dried coriander seeds, toasted

3 tablespoons palm sugar

3 kaffir lime leaves, julienned

6 large cloves garlic, crushed

2 stalks ground fresh lemongrass

3 large sprigs Thai basil, bruised, about 12 leaves

6 Thai chiles cut in rings or 3 serranos

5 tablespoons green curry paste (Mae Ploy brand)

¼ cup Viet Huong Fish Sauce (Three Crabs brand)

¼ cup concentrated pineapple juice

Zest of 2 limes

2½ pounds chicken wings, cut at the joint and rinsed in cold water

Place all the ingredients in a large bowl except chicken and mix well. Add the wings and marinate in refrigerator for 24 hours.

Place the wings and marinade in a large pot and gently bring to a simmer and cook slowly for 8 minutes. Remove the wings to a wire rack. Reduce the marinade by half, strain, and use to baste the wings while on the grill.

Preheat grill to medium and char the wings, basting with the green curry marinade until fully cooked. When ready to serve, sprinkle wings with Kaffir Lime Leaf Salt and serve with Lemongrass Mango Sauce, fresh cut mango chunks, and fresh Thai basil.

continued

KAFFIR LIME LEAF SALT

Makes ¼ cup

6 kaffir lime leaves, stems removed,
*   cut in fine julienne*
¼ cup coarse sea salt
Zest and juice of 1 kaffir lime

Place all the ingredients in a spice mill and pulse until well blended. This salt is great on shrimp and seafood as well.

LEMONGRASS MANGO SAUCE

Makes 2 cups

4 teaspoons minced lemongrass
4 green Thai bird's eye chiles, minced
2 ripe mangos
2 tablespoons palm sugar
Zest and juice of 2 limes
10 Thai basil leaves, julienned

In a medium saucepan, add lemongrass and chiles. Peel the mangos, remove the fruit from the pit, and add to the pan. To get the entire mango off the pit, use a grater on the biggest grate and press the pit against the grater; this will give a purée. Add the sugar and bring to a boil. Remove from heat, blend, strain, and cool. Add the lime zest and juice. Garnish wings with basil when ready to serve.

HOMEMADE GREEN THAI CURRY PASTE

Makes ¾ cup

2 cloves garlic
¾ teaspoon salt
2 tablespoons palm sugar
2 tablespoons dried whole shrimp
2 tablespoons minced shallot
4 tablespoons minced lemongrass
8 green Thai bird's eye chiles, minced
3 kaffir lime leaves, finely chopped
1 tablespoon grated galangal
1 teaspoon grated fresh turmeric
1½ teaspoons grated ginger
1 tablespoon sweet miso
1 teaspoon tamarind purée
½ bunch cilantro, roots only, minced
15 Thai basil leaves
3 tablespoons Viet Huong Fish Sauce
   (Three Crabs brand)

Peel the garlic and place in a large mortar, add the salt and smash until puréed; add the sugar. In a spice mill, grind the dried shrimp then add to the mortar, and continue to make a purée with the pestle. After each addition continue mashing, working on the sides of the mortar. Add the shallot, lemongrass, chiles, and lime leaves. Add the galangal, turmeric, and ginger. Finally, add the miso, tamarind purée, cilantro, basil, and fish sauce. Mix well.

Szechuan Chicken Wings

*China, Heat 8, **Serves 6***

Southern Chinese cooking style has bold flavors using garlic, chiles, and the famous tingling, numbing Szechuan peppercorn. The cuisine is composed of seven basic flavors: sour, pungent, hot, sweet, bitter, aromatic, and salty. Kung pao chicken, tea smoked duck, Chengdu-style hot pot stews, and Dandan noodles are favorites of the region. This recipe tries to give a taste of the region, so get something cold to drink. This one is hot. Allow 24 hours preparation time.

4 cups water

2 tablespoons salt

¼ cup honey

10 cloves garlic, crushed

4 green onions, chopped

1 (1-inch) piece fresh ginger, crushed

1 tablespoon Szechuan peppercorns

Zest and juice of 2 tangerines

2 tablespoons kecap manis
(ABC brand sweet soy sauce)

3 tablespoons double soy sauce

12 arbol chiles, toasted and crushed

2½ pounds chicken wings, cut at the joint and rinsed in cold water

Place water in a large saucepan, add the salt, honey, garlic, onions, ginger, peppercorns, tangerine zest and juice, kecap manis, double soy sauce, and chiles and bring to a boil for 5 minutes. Let cool completely before adding wings. Place the chicken in the brine to marinate for 12–24 hours in the refrigerator.

CHIU CHOW CHILE OIL

Makes 1½ cups

15 cloves garlic
1 tablespoon sesame oil
24 dried arbol chiles
1 cup soybean oil
3 tablespoons organic soy sauce
1 tablespoon toasted sesame oil
1 teaspoon salt, finely ground
1 teaspoon honey

Preheat oven to 375 degrees.

Place the garlic and sesame oil in a covered oven-proof pan and roast for 40 minutes. Remove from oven, mash the garlic, and set aside. Grind the chiles in a spice mill to flakes, larger pieces are preferred, about 4 tablespoons, and place in a small stainless steel bowl. Heat the soybean oil in a small saucepan to 375 degrees. Immediately, while the oil is still hot, add the garlic and pour over the ground chiles. Let the oil cool; add the soy sauce, sesame oil, salt, and honey. Mix well.

VELVET COATING

2 eggs
½ cup cornstarch
1 teaspoon salt
1 teaspoon sugar
1 teaspoon white pepper
½ teaspoon ground Szechwan peppercorns
2 cups peanut oil or rendered chicken fat

Preheat oven to 350 degrees.

Remove wings from brine and dry on paper towels. In a medium bowl, mix together eggs, cornstarch, salt, sugar, pepper, and peppercorns.

In a wok or deep fryer, heat oil to medium-high heat, about 375 degrees. Dip wings in Velvet Coating and place in hot oil, crisping the skin on all sides; cooking in batches for about 9 minutes each. Turn often and cook evenly until well browned. Remove and place on a wire rack on top of a baking sheet that has been lined with foil. Bake for 25 minutes.

continued

SZECHWAN STIR-FRY

1 cup Japanese chiles or arbol chiles

½ cup sliced green onions

2 cups diced red bell peppers

1 cup sliced celery heart, reserve leaves for garnish

2 tablespoons soy sauce

2 teaspoons kecap manis (ABC brand sweet soy sauce)

¼ cup tangerine juice or orange juice

2 tablespoons rice wine vinegar

1 tablespoon Chiu Chow Chile Oil or Lee Chum Chee brand

The key is to have all the ingredients measured and ready.

Remove all but 3 tablespoons of hot oil from the wok you just cooked the wings in, and fry the chiles until well toasted; remove from wok and reserve. Add the green onions, bell peppers, and celery to the hot wok and stir-fry, cooking very fast and hot. Add the soy sauce, kecap manis, tangerine juice, vinegar, and chile oil.

Add the cooked chicken and heat through if needed. Place on a large serving dish and garnish with roasted chiles and celery leaves. Serve with extra Chiu Chow Chile Oil.

Tebasaki Chicken Wings

Tebasaki refers to the flat, two-boned part of the wing. It is considered by the Japanese to be the perfect part of the chicken, because of its skin to meat ratio. These wings are pretty straightforward—dredged in a rice flour mixture and double fried. The interest is when they are dipped in the Miso Mayonnaise and combined with the pickled vegetables. Prepare the mayonnaise and vegetables first so you'll be ready when the wings come out. You'll notice that the recipe calls for MSG. It is naturally found in meat, fish, and milk and is a great flavor enhancer, so don't be afraid of it. If you don't want to use it, substitute a bit more salt. Allow 24 hours preparation time.

MISO MAYONNAISE

Makes 1 cup

1 cup mayonnaise
4 tablespoons white shiro miso
2 teaspoons sambal oelek
   (Asian chile paste)
Zest and juice of 1 orange

In a small bowl, combine the mayonnaise, miso, sambal oelek, zest and juice. Mix well.

PICKLED CUCUMBERS

Makes 1 cup

3 Japanese cucumbers
1 teaspoon salt
$\frac{1}{4}$ cup rice wine vinegar
2 tablespoons sugar
1 teaspoon toasted sesame oil

Cut the cucumbers in $\frac{1}{8}$-inch coins, place in a medium bowl, and add the salt. Let the cucumbers sit for 1 hour on the counter. Rinse in a colander under cold water and pat dry then place in a bowl. In a small saucepan, bring the vinegar, sugar, and sesame oil to a simmer, pour over the cucumbers, and refrigerate overnight.

continued

PICKLED RED MUSTARD GREENS

Makes 1 cup

1 bunch red mustard greens
½ teaspoon salt
1 teaspoon wasabi powder
⅓ cup rice wine vinegar
2 red Fresno chiles, chopped, with seeds

Cut the mustard greens in thin julienne strips and place in a medium bowl with the salt and wasabi powder. In a small saucepan, heat the vinegar and chiles to a simmer, pour over the mustard greens, cover, and refrigerate overnight.

WINGS

2½ pounds chicken wings, cut at the joint and rinsed in cold water
1½ teaspoons salt or Ajinomoto MSG powder
1½ teaspoons white pepper
1 tablespoon dried honey powder or brown sugar
2 tablespoons miso powder*
1 cup rice flour
1 tablespoon sancho (Sichuan pepper)

Preheat deep fryer to 260 degrees with the recommended amount of oil for your machine.

Place the wings in a large bowl and add the MSG, pepper, honey powder, miso powder, and flour. Coat completely and blanch the wings in the oil for 8 minutes. Remove the wings to a plate and heat the oil to 375 degrees. Fry the wings for 4 more minutes. Sprinkle with the sancho seasoning and serve with Miso Mayonnaise, Pickled Cucumbers, and Pickled Red Mustard Greens.

*Place a ¼ cup red miso on a piece of parchment paper, spread it out thin, and dry in a 200 degree oven for 1 hour. Grind to a powder.

Thai Sour Yellow Curry Wings

This recipe combines Indian-influenced spices with the rich coconut curry of Thailand. A key ingredient is the coconut cream, which is more concentrated and thicker than coconut milk. I encourage you to make your own cream (facing), but you can also buy it. Just be sure to look for "cream" on the label. Make sure you toast the spices before adding to the recipe, and fry the curry paste to release its flavors as you would in any Indian curry. Allow 12–24 hours preparation time.

2 green cardamom pods

½ teaspoon fennel seeds

2 teaspoons cumin seeds

2 tablespoons coconut oil

5 tablespoons yellow curry paste
  (Mae Ploy brand)

1 tablespoon salt

4 cups water

3 tablespoons palm sugar

3 kaffir lime leaves, julienned

3 tablespoons grated fresh turmeric
  or 5 teaspoons dried

6 large cloves garlic, thinly sliced

2 stalks fresh lemongrass, ground

4 red Thai chiles, cut in rings

3 tablespoons tamarind paste

¼ cup Viet Huong Fish Sauce
  (Three Crabs brand)

1 cup coconut cream*

Zest and juice of 2 limes

2½ pounds chicken wings, cut at the joint and
  rinsed in cold water

In a large 6-quart pot, toast the dried spices until fragrant over medium heat, about 2 minutes; make sure to crush the cardamom pods into smaller pieces. Add the coconut oil and yellow curry paste and fry for 1 additional minute. Add the salt and water and bring to a boil then remove from the heat and add the sugar, lime leaves, turmeric, garlic, lemongrass, chiles, tamarind paste, fish sauce, coconut cream, and lime zest and juice; mix well and let cool. Add the chicken wings and marinate in refrigerator for 12–24 hours.

Preheat grill to 350 degrees.

When ready to cook, bring the wings and marinade to a slow simmer in a large pot and cook over low heat for 8 minutes. Remove wings to a wire rack and reduce the marinade by half. Grill wings, basting with the marinade, for 12 minutes, until well charred and an internal temperature of 165–170 degrees is reached. Serve with Sweet Fresno Chile Dipping Sauce.

SWEET FRESNO CHILE DIPPING SAUCE

Makes 1½ cups

3 stalks lemongrass, roughly chopped
1 tablespoon chopped ginger
1 bruised kaffir lime leaf
6 tablespoons minced Fresno chiles
1 clove garlic, minced
2 tablespoons sambal oelek
   (Asian chile paste)
1½ cups water
¾ cup coconut sugar
½ cup concentrated pineapple juice
¼ cup honey

Place the lemongrass, ginger, and lime leaf in a cheesecloth and tie with a string. In a medium saucepan, mix together the chiles, garlic, sambal oelek, water, sugar, juice, and honey. Add cheesecloth pouch. Simmer for 10 minutes and then cool. Remove the cheesecloth when the sauce is cooled.

*Coconut cream is fresher and richer than coconut milk. If you have the desire to make your own, it's quite simple to make by using 1 fresh young coconut. Use a large knife to cut and remove the top portion of the coconut, reserve the water, and remove the coconut pulp. Purée the pulp in a blender with a small amount of coconut water and then strain it. This makes about 1 cup of cream.

Virginia Bacon Chicken Wings

There aren't many ingredients that add such a rich, smokey, crowd-pleasing flavor to almost anything as bacon. Wrapping the chicken wings in bacon takes them to a whole new level. We then finish them with a Burnt Onion Sauce, doubling down on the smokey flavor profile. Burnt sauces are very simple and flavorful ways to use vegetables as a replacement for heavy meat sauces. Roasting the onions until they are charred brings out the natural sugars, which are counterbalanced by the slight bitterness and smoke of the charred skin. Carrots, parsnips, and butternut squash are all great candidates for a similar treatment. So be adventurous and burn your food!

$2\frac{1}{2}$ pounds chicken drumettes,
   rinsed in cold water

2 teaspoons smoked salt

2 teaspoons pepper

2 tablespoons dried maple sugar granules

2 pounds center-cut smoked bacon

$\frac{1}{4}$ cup dried maple sugar granules

Preheat oven to 325 degrees.

Season the chicken with salt, pepper, and 2 tablespoons maple sugar. Place a half strip of bacon on a cutting board and sprinkle with maple sugar. Place a drumette on the bacon strip, roll it up, and secure with a toothpick. Repeat with remaining chicken and bacon. Place the wings on a wire rack on top of a baking sheet that has been covered with foil and bake for 40 minutes. Serve with Burnt Onion Sauce and Potato Salad.

continued

BURNT ONION SAUCE

Makes 3 cups

4 medium sweet Vidalia yellow onions
$\frac{1}{4}$ cup maple syrup or honey
2 cups chicken stock
1 sprig fresh thyme
1 tablespoon cracked black peppercorns
2 tablespoons balsamic vinegar

Preheat oven to 450 degrees.

Place the whole onions with skins on in a heavy-bottom pan and let roast for $1\frac{1}{2}$ hours. All the skin should look black. When the onions have cooled, cut into quarters and place in a medium saucepan, skins on, with the syrup, stock, thyme, peppercorns, and vinegar; simmer for 20 minutes. Pass sauce through a food mill or a medium grate strainer.

POTATO SALAD

Makes 6 servings

3 pounds russet potatoes
$1\frac{1}{2}$ teaspoons dry mustard
1 tablespoon whole grain mustard
1 tablespoon freshly ground black pepper
$\frac{1}{4}$ cup apple cider vinegar
$\frac{1}{4}$ cup maple syrup
1 cup diced white onion
6 hard-boiled eggs
$1\frac{1}{2}$ cups mayonnaise

Peel the potatoes and place in a large pot of salted water and boil for 20 minutes, or until tender. Let cool and dice into $\frac{1}{2}$-inch pieces. In a medium bowl, mix together the mustards, pepper, vinegar, syrup, and onion and pour over the potatoes. Rough chop the boiled eggs and add to potatoes. Mix in the mayonnaise and toss to coat, mixing well.

Buffalo Hot Wings

What's more classic than Buffalo wings? The secret to great Buffalo wings is the butter and the celery seeds in the sauce. If you prefer a less spicy sauce, reduce the dried chiles in the recipe. Use the Papillon brand of French Roquefort or Rogue Creamery Oregon Blue in the dipping sauce. It makes such a difference to the end result when you use quality ingredients. You can use the leftover cheese on salads or as a simple dessert with apples and Riesling. Allow 2 hours preparation time.

2 ½ *pounds chicken wings, cut at the joint*
  and rinsed in cold water

1 *tablespoon salt*

3 *tablespoons butter*

1 *clove garlic*

2 *tablespoons cayenne pepper*

1 *tablespoon whole pequin chiles*

12 *ounces V8 Spicy Hot Vegetable Juice*

¼ *cup chopped pickled red jalapeño*
  and carrots (La Casteno brand)

1 *tablespoon Sriracha Hot Chili Sauce*

½ *teaspoon salt*

¾ *teaspoon smoked salt*

¼ *cup ketchup*

1 *tablespoon tomato paste*

3 *tablespoons Tabasco Pepper Sauce*

¼ *cup Tabasco Habañero Sauce*

¼ *cup white vinegar*

⅛ *teaspoon pepper*

¼ *teaspoon celery seeds*

Place the wings in a large bowl and add 1 tablespoon salt; toss to coat. Let the wings brine for 2 hours in the refrigerator. Remove wings and dry with paper towels.

In a medium saucepan, heat the butter and garlic, letting the butter brown on low temperature. Add the cayenne and pequin chiles and let cook for 30 seconds. Add the juice, pickled jalapeño and carrots, Sriracha, ½ teaspoon salt, smoked salt, ketchup, tomato paste, Pepper Sauce, Habañero Sauce, vinegar, pepper, and celery seeds; bring to a boil. Remove from heat, purée in a blender, and strain. Set aside.

Preheat deep fryer to 260 degrees with the recommended amount of oil for your machine. Cook the wings slowly for 12 minutes. Remove wings to a plate and heat the oil to 375 degrees. Place wings back in oil and crisp the skins for 4 minutes. Remove wings to a bowl and toss with as much sauce as you desire. Serve with Yogurt Blue Cheese Dip, carrot, celery, and bell pepper spears.

continued

YOGURT BLUE CHEESE DIP

Makes 1¼ cups

¾ cup Greek-style yogurt or sour cream
¼ cup crumbled Roquefort (Papillon)
2 tablespoons mayonnaise
1 tablespoon buttermilk
⅛ teaspoon salt
¼ teaspoon pepper
1 clove garlic, sliced very thin

In a small bowl, mix all ingredients together until well combined. Refrigerate any leftovers.

Cajun Blackened Chicken Wings

Classic Cajun cooking has a spicy, multi-cultural flavor profile that incorporates garlic, peppers, onions, and spices like cayenne and paprika. We "blacken" these wings by searing them in the spices. Then we top them off with a rich remoulade sauce that is similar to Russian dressing, but with the added zing of more spices and andouille sausage. Serve wings with the Shrimp, Corn, and Potato Salad that mimics the ingredients of a classic shrimp boil—corn, potatoes, gumbo spices, and of course shrimp. Put a little New Orleans jazz on and you have yourself a party! Allow 2 hours preparation time.

CAJUN SPICE MIX

2 tablespoons kosher salt

¼ cup Hungarian paprika

2 tablespoons coarsely ground black pepper

4 teaspoons garlic powder

4 teaspoons onion powder

4 teaspoons cayenne pepper

2 teaspoons oregano

2 teaspoons dried thyme

2 teaspoons chipotle powder

2½ pounds chicken wings, cut at the joint and rinsed in cold water

In a small bowl, combine all ingredients except chicken. Place the wings in a medium bowl and coat with half the spice mix. Marinate in refrigerator for 2 hours.

Preheat oven to 300 degrees.

Place the wings on a wire rack on top of a baking sheet that has been covered with foil and bake for 35 minutes. Remove from oven and coat with the remaining spice mix, reserving 1 tablespoon for the remoulade and 2 teaspoons for the potato salad.

Preheat a large cast iron pan on medium high and sear the wings in batches. Clean the pan out after each batch with a paper towel to remove any burnt spices. Serve with Remoulade and Shrimp, Corn, and Potato Salad.

continued

REMOULADE

Makes 3 cups

2 tablespoons butter
4 ounces diced andouille sausage
½ cup diced red bell pepper
½ cup diced green bell pepper
½ cup diced white onion
¼ cup diced celery
6 cloves garlic, thinly sliced
1 tablespoon Cajun Spice Mix
3 tablespoons bourbon
2 tablespoons white balsamic vinegar
¼ cup tomato paste
¼ cup Louisiana hot sauce
½ cup mayonnaise
2 tablespoons Zatarain's Creole Mustard
4 green onions, thinly sliced

In a medium saucepan, heat the butter and sausage. Add the bell peppers, onion, celery, garlic, and spice mix and sweat until the vegetables are golden brown. Add the bourbon and vinegar to deglaze pan. Add the tomato paste and hot sauce, mixing well. Remove from heat and let mixture cool before adding mayonnaise, mustard, and onions.

SHRIMP, CORN, AND POTATO SALAD

Makes 6 servings

1 pound red potatoes
1 teaspoon salt
3 cups yellow corn
1 teaspoon gumbo filé spice
2 teaspoons Cajun Spice Mix
1 pound small shrimp, peeled and deveined
4 pickled red jalapeño peppers, diced
½ cup crème fraîche

Cut the potatoes in ¼-inch pieces and place in a large pot with enough water to cover. Add the salt and cook, covered, for 20 minutes over medium-high heat. Remove all but 1 cup of water then add the corn, gumbo filé, and spice mix, continue to cook for 5 minutes more. Add the shrimp and cook for 2 minutes. Remove from heat and place potato mixture on a baking sheet and cool in refrigerator. When cool, add the jalapeños and crème fraîche. Mix well to coat.

Fiery Habañero Wings

These wings pack a punch! They juxtapose the fiery habañeros and Mayan achiote paste with the bright citric flavors of orange, lemon, lime, and pineapple. This recipe originated in the Yucatan, where citrus flavors are used throughout the cuisine. The achiote paste is made from annatto seeds, which have the flavor of slightly peppery nutmeg. Allow 4–6 hours preparation time.

2 teaspoons salt

1 teaspoon dried habañero powder

½ teaspoon citric acid

3 habañero chiles, minced

Zest and juice of 1 orange

Zest and juice of 1 lemon

2 tablespoons concentrated orange juice

*3 tablespoons achiote paste
(El Yucateco brand)*

6 cloves garlic, roasted and puréed

*2½ pounds chicken wings, cut at the joint
and rinsed in cold water*

In a spice mill or small blender, add the salt, habañero powder, citric acid, chiles, zest and juices, achiote paste, and garlic to make a paste.

Place chicken in a medium bowl and add paste, tossing to coat. Marinate wings in refrigerator for 4–6 hours.

Preheat oven to 350 degrees. Place the wings on a wire rack on top of a baking sheet that has been covered with foil. Bake for 35 minutes, or until an internal temperature of 165–170 degrees is reached. Serve with Pineapple Habañero Glaze.

PINEAPPLE HABAÑERO GLAZE

Makes 1½ cups

1 tablespoon canola oil
1 orange bell pepper, seeds removed, diced
4 habañero chiles, sliced in half, stems removed
½ teaspoon salt
½ cup concentrated pineapple juice
¼ cup agave nectar
2 tablespoons lime juice

In a medium saucepan, add oil, bell pepper, and chiles; cook over medium-low heat until slightly brown, about 5 minutes. Add the salt, juice, and nectar; cover and cook for 5 minutes on a low simmer. Remove from heat and cool completely. When cool, place in a blender and purée; add the lime juice.

West Texas Smokey Wings

Texas has four distinct styles of barbecue. East Texas likes a sweet tomato-based sauce; Central Texas uses a spice rub; South Texas inhabitants favor a thick molasses sauce; and my favorite, is the West Texas style that is super smokey. These wings get their rich smokiness from the marinade, the sauce, and the cooking method. Ingredients such as chipotle chiles (smoked jalapeños), smoked salt, cumin, and liquid smoke all provide layers of different smokey flavors. And the grilling over mesquite finishes these wings off with that unique cowboy flare. Allow 24 hours preparation time.

SMOKEY BRINE

1 head garlic

1 onion

4 cups water

2 tablespoons kosher salt

1 tablespoon smoked salt

¼ cup brown sugar

2 bay leaves

1 tablespoon black peppercorns, toasted and crushed

4 chipotle peppers, toasted and crushed

1 (7-ounce) can chipotle en adobo, puréed

1 tablespoon ground cumin, roasted

1 ounce fresh thyme

½ teaspoon pecan liquid smoke

2½ pounds whole chicken wings, rinsed in cold water

In a heavy-bottom cast iron pan, dry roast the garlic and onions over medium-high heat for 15 minutes, or until well roasted and blackened. Place the garlic and onions in a large saucepan with water, salt, smoked salt, sugar, bay leaves, peppercorns, chipotles, chipotle en adobo, cumin, thyme, and liquid smoke. Bring to a boil for 5 minutes and cool completely before adding the chicken. Place wings and brine in a large bowl and marinate in refrigerator for 12–24 hours. Remove wings from the brine and place on a wire rack.

Preheat a grill with mesquite charcoal to medium heat and cook the wings over indirect heat for 25 minutes. Baste wings with West Texas Barbecue Sauce and char well over direct heat; serve with remaining sauce, Esquites (Creamy Corn Cups), and Smokey Black Beans.

continued

WEST TEXAS BARBECUE SAUCE

Makes 3 cups

6–8 chipotle morita chiles, stemmed
4 cups water
12 ounces dark beer
2 cloves garlic
1 small white onion, peeled and sliced
¼ cup cherry tomatoes
1 tablespoon tomato paste
4 teaspoons ketchup
1 tablespoon Tabasco Chipotle Pepper Sauce
½ teaspoon kosher salt
¾ teaspoon smoked salt
2 tablespoons brown sugar
1 teaspoon ground cumin
2 teaspoons coriander
½ teaspoon oregano, toasted
¼ cup sherry vinegar

In a heavy-bottom cast iron pan, toast chiles for 2 minutes over medium-high heat. Place chiles in a large saucepan with the water and beer; cook uncovered for 20 minutes or until 2 cups of liquid is left. Place in a blender. In same pan, roast the garlic and onion for 12 minutes and add to the blender. Increase the heat to medium high and dry roast the tomatoes until blackened and add to the blender. Purée ingredients for 4 minutes on medium speed. Place purée in a medium saucepan and add the tomato paste, ketchup, Tabasco, salt, smoked salt, sugar, cumin, coriander, oregano, and vinegar and heat to a boil and cook for 2 minutes.

ESQUITES (CREAMY CORN CUPS)

Makes 6 servings

6 ears sweet yellow corn, husked and silks
    removed
6 tablespoons Mexican créma
6 tablespoons butter, melted
Pinch salt
6 tablespoons crumbled queso fresco
2 teaspoons ground New Mexican
    red chile powder
6 lime wedges

Bring a large saucepan of salted water to a boil and cook the corn for 5–7 minutes. Remove the corn and let cool slightly. Cut the kernels from the cobs, making sure not to cut too deep into the cob. Place the corn in a medium bowl and add the créma, butter, and salt and divide the corn into six individual serving cups. Sprinkle with cheese and chile powder and garnish with a lime wedge.

SMOKEY BLACK BEANS

Makes 6 servings

1 pound dry black beans, rinsed
9 cups water
2 medium onions, diced, divided
6 cloves garlic, roasted
1 sprig fresh thyme
1 tablespoon ground cumin, toasted
4 chipotle chiles, toasted and seeded
2 teaspoons smoked salt
5 Roma tomatoes
⅓ cup olive oil
3 chipotle morita chiles, stemmed and seeded
3 tablespoons dried avocado leaves or fresh,
   if available
¼ cup diced chipotle chiles en adobo,
   without seeds
2 tablespoons tomato paste

Place the beans, water, half of the onions, garlic, thyme, cumin, and chipotle chiles in a large stock pot and cook covered for 2 hours. Add the salt when the beans are tender. Remove chiles from the beans, dice, and reserve.

Heat a large heavy-bottom cast iron pan to high and blacken the tomatoes for 12 minutes. Remove from heat and set aside. Heat oil in the same pan and sauté the onion, morita chiles, and avocado leaves until golden brown. Add to a blender along with tomatoes and 3 cups of bean cooking liquid. Purée and add to the beans. Add the reserved diced chipotles and tomato paste and cook for an additional 15 minutes.

Jalapeño Hot Wings

Jalapeño wing recipes typically are served with store-bought jelly, so I included a recipe for jalapeño jelly as an upgrade. This recipe is fresher and replaces the jelly with a cheese dipping sauce, which takes it over the top as a great sports and party food. It's almost like spicy chicken wing fondue. Serve with plenty of warm flour tortillas and remember—the mess is half the fun! Allow 4 hours preparation time.

2 tablespoons dried oregano, toasted

¼ cup olive oil

¼ cup lime juice

4 jalapeño peppers, with seeds

2 cloves garlic

2 teaspoons salt

1 teaspoon dried jalapeño powder
   (North of the Border Chili Co.)

1 bunch cilantro, without stems

2 tablespoons fresh oregano

2½ pounds chicken wings, cut at the joint
   and rinsed in cold water

Place dried oregano, oil, lime juice, jalapeños, garlic, salt, jalapeño powder, cilantro, and fresh oregano in a blender and blend until smooth.

Place chicken in a medium bowl and toss with marinade to coat. Marinate wings in refrigerator for up to 4 hours, but no longer as the lime juice breaks down the protein and makes it too soft.

Preheat oven to 375 degrees. Place the wings on a wire rack on top of a baking sheet that has been covered with foil. Bake for 25 minutes then pan fry in a nonstick frying pan for 6–8 minutes to crisp the skin. Serve with Jalapeño Fundido and Jalapeño Jelly on the side.

continued

JALAPEÑO FUNDIDO

Makes 6 servings

1 onion, thinly sliced
2 tablespoons Tabasco Jalapeño Green
　　Pepper Sauce
8 jalapeño peppers
12 ounces grated jalapeño jack cheese
4 ounces Mexican crema
1 teaspoon dried coriander

Preheat oven to 350 degrees.

In a heavy-bottom cast iron pan, dry roast onion over medium heat for 12 minutes; remove and place in an 8 x 8-inch baking dish. Sprinkle green pepper sauce over the onions.

In same pan, dry roast jalapeños over medium heat for 12 minutes. Place in a plastic bag and let steam until cooled. Peel, deseed, and cut into thin strips; reserve.

Evenly layer cheese over top of roasted onions and pour crema over cheese. Place a layer of jalapeño strips over cheese and dust with coriander. Bake for 12–15 minutes, or until cheese melts.

JALAPEÑO JELLY

Makes 3 cups

1 poblano pepper
5 jalapeño peppers
¾ cup apple cider vinegar
2¼ cups sugar
1 tablespoon jalapeño powder
1 ounce liquid pectin
5 jalapeño peppers, roasted, peeled, seeded,
　　and diced in ⅛-inch pieces
¼ teaspoon sea salt

In a food processor chop the poblano and jalapeños into fine pieces. Place in a large saucepan with vinegar and sugar and bring to a boil. Cook for 8 minutes, stirring occasionally. Remove and strain mixture. Return strained mixture to saucepan and add the jalapeño powder, pectin, roasted jalapeños, and salt; simmer for 5 minutes, stirring occasionally. Place jelly in small jars and continue with canning process, if desired. However, the jelly is best eaten and served fresh. Refrigerate leftovers.

African Piri Piri Wings

Piri Piri is Swahili for "pepper pepper" and is what we call the African bird's eye chile. It grows in Malawi, Ghana, Nigeria, and Zimbabwe and made its way to Portugal with Columbus. About 1000 years ago, Arabs settled in the coastal areas of east Africa and influenced Swahili cuisine with the use of saffron, cloves, cinnamon, and fruit. Later influences include India with spices such as coriander, cardamom, and cumin. This recipe includes all of the above and truly reflects the eclectic tastes of the region.

BERBERE SPICE MIX

3½ tablespoons coriander seeds

2½ teaspoons cumin seeds

2 teaspoons fennel seeds

½ teaspoon fenugreek seeds

¾ teaspoon ajwain seeds

½ teaspoon black peppercorns

¾ teaspoon mace

7 green cardamom seeds

1 teaspoon cinnamon

4 allspice berries

3 cloves

2 teaspoons salt

2½ pounds chicken wings, cut at the joint and rinsed in cold water

Preheat oven to 375 degrees.

Place spices except salt in a small nonstick frying pan over low heat and toast for 1–2 minutes, or until fragrant, stirring frequently. Use caution as these dried ingredients can scorch easily, causing bitterness. Place toasted spices in a mortar or spice mill along with the salt and grind to a powder.

Place the wings in a medium bowl, add the spice mix and toss to coat; marinate for 1 hour in the refrigerator.

Place the wings on a wire rack on top of a baking sheet lined with foil and bake for 30–35 minutes, or until golden brown and an internal temperature of 165–170 degrees is reached. Serve with Piri Piri Chile Sauce.

continued

NITER KIBBEH (ETHIOPIAN SPICED BUTTER)

Makes ¾ cup

1 cup butter
¼ teaspoon black cardamom seeds
¼ teaspoon fenugreek powder
¼ teaspoon ground nigella seeds
*   (onion seeds)*

Heat the butter in a small saucepan over medium-low heat and bring to a low simmer skimming the foam off the surface. Continue skimming the milk solids from the top for about 20 minutes until the butter is completely clear. Stir in the cardamom, fenugreek, and nigella seeds. Cool and transfer to an airtight container. Keep refrigerated.

PIRI PIRI CHILE SAUCE

Makes 2 cups

¼ cup chopped onion
3 cloves garlic, chopped
1 teaspoon grated fresh ginger
3 tablespoons Niter Kibbeh
*   (Ethiopian Spiced Butter)*
2 tablespoons ground piri piri
1 teaspoon paprika dulce
1½ cups V8 Spicy Hot Vegetable Juice
2 tablespoons tomato paste
1½ teaspoons salt
¼ cup white vinegar
2 tablespoons lemon juice
1 tablespoon Sriracha Hot Chili Sauce

In a medium saucepan, heat the onion, garlic, ginger, and butter and cook slowly for 7 minutes. Add the piri piri and paprika and cook for an additional 2 minutes. Add the juice, tomato paste, and salt and cook for 5 minutes. Add mixture to a blender and purée. Add the vinegar, lemon juice, and chili sauce. Mix well.

Chick Pea Battered Wings

Chick peas (garbanzo beans) are among the legumes that are highest in protein and are one of the earliest cultivated foods, dating back 7,500 years. In this recipe, they are incorporated into the batter of these spicy wings. I've also included a recipe for Turkish Tomatoes that goes great as a side dish. The tomatoes are seasoned with sumac, an ingredient with a tart, citrus flavor that can replace lemon or lime. It is frequently used in Middle-Eastern dishes, added to rice, sprinkled on kabobs, tossed in salads, and used as a garnish for hummus. Allow 12 hours preparation time.

BASIC GREEN CHILE BRINE

4 cups water

3 tablespoons kosher salt

2 tablespoons sugar

1 bay leaf

10 large cloves garlic, skin on, crushed

2 tablespoons coriander seeds, toasted

¼ cup dried green chile caribe
  (North of the Border Chile Co.)

3 jalapeño peppers, cut in half

1 teaspoon dried jalapeño powder
  (North of the Border Chile Co.)

1 ounce fresh oregano

1 heaping tablespoon dried oregano,
  toasted

½ bunch cilantro, chopped

Zest of 4 limes

2½ pounds chicken wings, cut at the joint
  and rinsed in cold water

Place all ingredients except chicken in a large saucepan and bring to a boil for 5 minutes. Remove from heat and let cool completely.

Place cooled brine and wings in a large bowl and marinate for 12 hours in the refrigerator.

Place the brine and wings in a large pot and bring to a simmer for 8 minutes to parcook the wings. Remove wings and let cool on a wire rack until ready to batter and fry.

continued

GARBANZO BEAN BATTER

2 cups garbanzo bean flour
2 cloves garlic, peeled and mashed
1 teaspoon salt
1 teaspoon cumin
2 teaspoons coriander
1 (12-ounce) can beer

Preheat deep fryer to 350 degrees with the recommended amount of oil for your machine.

In a medium bowl, mix together the flour, garlic, salt, cumin, coriander, and beer to make a thin batter. Dip the partially cooked wings in the batter and deep fry for 6 minutes in batches. Serve with Turkish Tomatoes.

TURKISH TOMATOES

Makes 3 cups

8 Roma tomatoes
4 cloves garlic, thinly sliced
1 teaspoon chopped thyme
1 teaspoon coriander
½ teaspoon cumin
2 teaspoons sugar
1 teaspoon salt
3 tablespoons sumac, divided
2 tablespoons olive oil
6 jalapeño peppers
1 teaspoon cured lemon or fresh lemon zest
3 tablespoons chopped Italian parsley
1 tablespoon lemon olive oil

Preheat oven to 225 degrees.

Prepare an ice bath and a large pot of boiling water. With a sharp knife, cut an X on the bottom of the tomatoes and remove the core. Blanch 4 tomatoes at a time, for 10–15 seconds, in the boiling water and then place directly in the ice bath. Peel and cut the tomatoes in half. Place tomatoes in a medium bowl with the garlic, thyme, coriander, cumin, sugar, salt, 2 tablespoons sumac, and olive oil. Toss to coat. Place tomatoes on a baking sheet lined with parchment paper cut side down and oven dry for 2 hours. Remove from oven, roughly chop, and place in a medium bowl. Fire roast the jalapeños over an open flame and place in a plastic bag to steam. When cooled, peel, seed, and finely chop. Add with remaining sumac, zest, lemon, parsley, and oil to tomatoes; toss to combine.

Greek God Wings

Remember, there are several Greek gods with wings! Nike, the winged goddess personified strength, speed, and victory. Mercury wore winged sandals and was god of commerce, trade, and travel. This Greek-inspired wing recipe is based on dolmas, the stuffed grape leaves. A rice mixture infused with the flavors of Greece—lemon, mint, cumin, and even ouzo—is wrapped inside a grape leaf along with the chicken. The wings are finished off with a delicious yogurt feta dipping sauce that uses sorrel, a sour herb, to really get the sauce flying. If you can't find sorrel, watercress is an acceptable substitute.

2½ pounds chicken drumettes, rinsed in cold water

2 teaspoons salt

1 teaspoon pepper

1 tablespoon dried oregano

3 tablespoons olive oil

1 (24-ounce) jar grape leaves, drained and veined (removing the back edges of the leaves' fibrous membrane with a small knife)

½ cup water or chicken stock

¼ cup ouzo

Place the drumettes, salt, pepper, oregano, and oil in a medium bowl, tossing to coat, and marinate in refrigerator for 1 hour.

Preheat a large nonstick frying pan on high heat and sear the drumettes until golden brown. Remove from pan and let cool.

Preheat oven to 375 degrees.

Place 1 heaping tablespoon of Stuffing, (page 56), into center of a grape leaf and top with a drumette. Fold in the sides of the grape leaf and roll into a little cigar shape. Continue until all are wrapped. Place the wrapped grape leaves in a nonstick baking dish, adding the water and ouzo. Bake, covered, for 30 minutes. Served with Yogurt, Feta Cheese, and Sorrel Dip.

continued

STUFFING

Makes 3½ cups

2 white onions, peeled and minced

2 tablespoons olive oil

1 teaspoon salt

1½ cups basmati rice

2 tablespoons pine nuts

3 tablespoons currants

1 tablespoon tomato paste

1 tablespoon lemon peel

2 tablespoons chopped fresh mint
   or 1 tablespoon dried

2 tablespoons fresh dill weed
   or 1 tablespoon dried

1 tablespoon cinnamon

1 teaspoon allspice

1 teaspoon cumin

2½ cups water

¼ cup ouzo

In a large frying pan, sauté the onions in oil for 4 minutes, or until golden. Add the salt, rice, pine nuts, currants, tomato paste, lemon peel, mint, dill, cinnamon, allspice, cumin, water, and ouzo and cook, covered, for 12 minutes, or until the liquid is absorbed and the rice is tender. Let mixture cool.

YOGURT, FETA CHEESE, AND SORREL DIP

Makes 1¼ cups

¾ cup Greek-style yogurt

¼ cup crumbled sheep milk feta

3 tablespoons julienned sorrel

2 tablespoons olive oil

1 clove garlic, thinly sliced

1 tablespoon buttermilk

⅛ teaspoon salt

¼ teaspoon pepper

In a small bowl, combine the yogurt, feta, sorrel, oil, garlic, and buttermilk. Mix well to combine. Season with salt and pepper.

Moroccan Green Charmoula Wings

These wings are all about the flavor of ras el hanout, *a spice mixture that literally means "top of the shop," or the best the purveyor has to offer. It can contain as many as 30 different spices, and every spice shop in Morocco has a secret combination they have perfected over the years. Making your own can seem daunting, but with a little organization, a good shopping list, and a spice grinder, it is well worth the effort. If you do buy the premade* ras el hanout, *simply toast it for 1 minute in a dry pan to freshen it and add any other spices you think will improve it. I always recommend adding more spice after the cooking process to keep the flavors fresher.*

RAS EL HANOUT

Makes ½ cup

3 tablespoons coriander seeds
5 teaspoons cumin seeds
2 teaspoons dried orange peel
2 teaspoons fennel seeds
1 teaspoon whole grains of paradise
14 allspice berries
½ teaspoon caraway seeds
2 teaspoons green cardamom seeds
½ teaspoon black peppercorns
2 black cardamom pods, seeds removed
2 Balinese long peppers
¾ teaspoon mace
2 arbol chiles
1 teaspoon ground cinnamon
8 whole cloves
½ piece star anise

Measure and place all the ingredients you will need on a plate. In a medium nonstick frying pan heated to medium low, toast all the ingredients for 3–4 minutes or until you can smell the fragrance of the spices. This releases the oils in the spices. Once you have reached this point return the spices to the plate so that they don't continue to cook.

Whole spices you won't toast:

1⅛ teaspoons yellow mustard seed
2 teaspoons dried rosebuds
½ teaspoon brown mustard seed
2 teaspoons granulated garlic
2¼ teaspoons ground ginger
½ nutmeg, grated
½ teaspoon citric acid

continued

Place the untoasted spices with the toasted spices in a spice or coffee mill and grind until fine.

2½ pounds chicken wings, cut at the joint and
   rinsed in cold water
2 teaspoons salt
⅓ cup Ras el Hanout, or more to taste

Preheat oven to 400 degrees.

Place the wings in a tagine with the salt and the Ras el Hanout. Cover and cook for 45 minutes. Add more Ras el Hanout after the wings have been cooked. Serve with Green Charmoula.

GREEN CHARMOULA

Makes 2 cups

2 poblano chiles
1 cup chopped green tomato
1 tablespoon kosher salt
1 tablespoon dried green chile powder
1 teaspoon smoked paprika
1 teaspoon ground cumin
1 teaspoon pepper
2 tablespoons minced garlic
½ cup coarsely chopped flat-leaf parsley

½ cup coarsely chopped cilantro
½ cup coarsely chopped mint
2 tablespoons chopped preserved lemon rind
Juice of 1 lemon
¼ cup olive oil
¼ cup honey

Over an open flame, fire roast the poblanos until well charred. Place in a plastic bag to steam. When cool, peel and seed, then place in a food processor with the tomatoes, salt, chile powder, paprika, cumin, pepper, garlic, parsley, cilantro, mint, lemon, oil, and honey; process until well chopped, but not puréed.

Pomegranate Chicken Wings

Pomegranate glazes are very common in Persian cuisine and lend themselves to these slightly tart, slightly sweet wings. Juicing a pomegranate is much easier than you think. Gently push the skin of the whole fruit in toward the center until it yields to the touch, being careful not to break the skin. Repeat by working around the fruit until it feels like a soft ball. Use a paring knife and make an incision so that the juice can flow out. It is the perfect portable juice box. Allow 12 hours preparation time.

2 cups water

2 cups pomegranate juice

¾ cup pomegranate molasses

1 tablespoon salt

2 teaspoons turmeric

2 tablespoons Hungarian hot paprika

1 tablespoon pepper

3 tablespoons sumac

1 onion, peeled and grated

2½ pounds chicken wings, cut at the joint and rinsed in cold water

In a large bowl, mix all the ingredients together. Place in refrigerator and marinate wings for 12 hours.

Place the wings and marinade in a large pot and bring to a simmer for 8 minutes. Remove wings and strain the marinade. Place marinade back in pot and reduce by half over medium-high heat. Remove from heat and set aside.

Preheat oven to 350 degrees.

Place the wings on a wire rack on top of a baking sheet lined with foil. Place in oven and roast for 30 minutes, or until internal temperature of 165–170 degrees is reached. Baste with reduced marinade. The sugar in the pomegranate molasses will burn if using a grill, so use indirect heat and just finish over the fire at the last minute. Serve with Yogurt Dip and Roasted Red Pepper Dip.

continued

YOGURT DIP

Makes 1½ cups

2 shallots, peeled and finely minced
1 cup water
1½ cups plain yogurt
½ teaspoon salt
½ teaspoon pepper
1 tablespoon chopped fresh tarragon

In a small bowl, add the shallots and water and let sit for 10 minutes; drain. In a separate bowl, mix together the shallots, yogurt, salt, pepper, and tarragon. Refrigerate any leftovers.

ROASTED RED PEPPER DIP

Makes 3 cups

4 red bell peppers
4 Fresno chiles
¾ cup walnuts
½ teaspoon cumin seeds
1 white onion, peeled and diced
½ cup olive oil, divided
2 tablespoons breadcrumbs
4 tablespoons pomegranate molasses
½ teaspoon salt
½ cup pomegranate seeds
1 pomegranate, juiced

Preheat oven to 475 degrees.

With the broiler turned on, place a rack just above center of the oven. Roast the bell peppers and chiles for 12 minutes, turning to blister the skins. Place them in a plastic bag to let steam. When cooled, peel and remove seeds. Dice 1 bell pepper and 1 chile; place in a small bowl and set aside.

Reduce oven temperature to 300 degrees and toast the walnuts and cumin seeds for 10 minutes; remove from oven and reserve. In a small frying pan, sauté the onion in ¼ cup oil, until golden brown. In a food processor, place the remaining peppers, chiles, walnuts, onions, ¼ cup oil, breadcrumbs, molasses, and salt; purée. Fold in the reserved diced pepper, diced chile, pomegranate seeds, and pomegranate juice.

Mole Verde Chicken Wings

The classic pipian verde is made with pumpkin seeds, but a sister recipe known as mole verde is made without. The convent of Santa Rosa in Puebla, Mexico, famous for its pipian verde, was the heart of experimental cuisine for Mexico. The nuns, daughters of colonial-era Puebla aristocrats, turned the convents into laboratories of gastronomy. The kitchens produced creative and daring mixtures of indigenous and traditional Spanish ingredients. Mole verde, just one of the seven famous moles in Mexico, is a green-chile-based sauce that pairs well with richer foods; whereas the pipian verde is more suited to leaner cuts of meat. Allow 12–24 hours preparation time.

BASIC GREEN CHILE BRINE

4 cups water
3 tablespoons kosher salt
2 tablespoons sugar
1 bay leaf
10 cloves garlic, skin on, crushed
2 tablespoons toasted coriander seeds
¼ cup dried green chile caribe
    (North of the Border Chile Co.)
3 jalapeño peppers, cut in half with seeds
1 teaspoon dried jalapeño powder
    (North of the Border Chile Co.)
1 ounce fresh oregano
1 heaping tablespoon dried oregano,
    toasted
½ bunch chopped cilantro
Zest of 4 limes
2½ pounds chicken wings, cut at the joint
    and rinsed in cold water

In a medium pot, add the water, salt, sugar, bay leaf, garlic, coriander, chile caribe, jalapeños, jalapeño powder, oregano, and dried oregano; bring to a boil. Remove from heat and cool in an ice bath until completely cold. Add the cilantro, lime zest and chicken wings. Marinate in refrigerator for 12–24 hours.

Preheat oven to 375 degrees and a deep fryer if using.

Remove wings from the brine and place on a wire rack on top of a baking sheet that has been lined with foil. Roast for 30–35 minutes, or until an internal temperature of 165–170 degrees is reached. The wings can be fried for 3 minutes to crisp the skin or roasted in the oven for a total of 40 minutes.

continued

VERDE MOLE

Makes 4 cups

6 medium tomatillos
4 poblano peppers, roasted
3 jalapeño peppers, roasted
1 cup chicken stock
2 cups chopped romaine
½ cup chopped cilantro, leaves only
½ teaspoon cumin seed, toasted
1 teaspoon coriander seed, toasted
¼ teaspoon anise seed, toasted
½ teaspoon salt
1 yellow corn tortilla, dried in oven
2 teaspoons fresh tarragon
6 large basil leaves
2 tablespoons corn oil

Husk the tomatillos and wash 5 times in hot water. In a medium pot of boiling water, blanch the tomatillos for 4 minutes. Place tomatillos in a blender with the peppers, stock, romaine, cilantro, cumin, coriander, anise, salt, tortilla, tarragon, and basil. Purée for 3 minutes or until a very smooth sauce is achieved.

Heat the oil in a large, deep frying pan to just barely the smoking point, add the sauce all at once and fry for 3–5 minutes. Use as a dipping sauce for the wings.

If you feel like making the pipian verde, simply toast 1 pound of pumpkin seeds, 9 ounces of peanuts, and ¾ cup sesame seeds and add to this recipe; blend until smooth. Serve with turkey, pork loin, or chicken breast.

Amarillo Chicken Wings

No, these wings aren't from Amarillo, Texas. They get their name from the Oaxacan yellow mole used. (Amarillo means "yellow" in Spanish.) The yellow mole is one of the famous seven moles of Oaxaca. Moles are rich, complex sauces that flavor meat stews and incorporate many ingredients and spices to create layers upon layers of flavor. This version is a bit simpler. This mole is more reddish than yellow and has a brighter, fresher flavor thanks to the use of pineapple inspired by the Yucatan region. Allow 2 hours preparation time.

AMARILLO SAUCE

Makes 4 cups

2 small white onions, peeled and cut in half
4 cloves garlic
4 habañero peppers, cut in half, with seeds
2 tablespoons olive oil
12 guero chiles, stemmed, roughly chopped
2 pounds yellow tomatoes, cored
2 orange bell peppers, stemmed, seeded, roughly chopped
½ golden pineapple, peeled, core removed, and quartered
2 teaspoons salt
2 teaspoons sugar
1 teaspoon white balsamic vinegar
2 teaspoons white vinegar

Preheat oven to 450 degrees.

Place the onions, garlic, and habañeros on a sheet of parchment paper or aluminum foil; add the olive oil. Fold the paper in half, creating a pyramid shape. Folding the edges, start from one end, continue to the opposite end, and fold each fold over the last, creating a seal. Finish by tucking the end fold under the parcel. Bake for 30 minutes.

Place chiles, tomatoes, and bell peppers in a baking dish and bake for 40 minutes, uncovered.

Place the pineapple on a baking sheet and bake for 40 minutes.

In a blender, place the onions, garlic, and habañeros, guero chiles, tomatoes, bell pepper, and roasted pineapple. Blend and finish with salt, sugar, balsamic and white vinegars. Use half of the sauce to marinate the wings, and the other half as a dipping sauce.

continued

WINGS

2½ pounds chicken wings, cut at the joint and
*   rinsed in cold water*
2 teaspoons salt
4 allspice berries, ground
4 cloves, ground
½ recipe Amarillo Sauce

Place wings, salt, allspice, cloves, and Amarillo Sauce in a large bowl. Toss to coat and marinate in refrigerator for 2 hours.

Preheat oven to 375 degrees.

Place wings on a wire rack on top of a baking sheet covered with foil and bake for 25–30 minutes, basting with the marinade every 10 minutes. Cook until golden brown and an internal temperature of 170 degrees is reached. Serve with the remaining Amarillo Sauce.

Carnival Wings

The world famous Carnival in Rio de Janeiro is the great festival held right before Lent. It's the last chance for everyone to go a little crazy before they say farewell to bad habits and practice repentance during the Lenten season leading up to Easter. Huge parades are led by samba schools; the costumes vary from one region to the next and depict unique cultural and local folklore. These wings reflect the Caribbean side of Brazil's many cultures with the tropical flavors of brown sugar, lime, and mint.

2 ½ pounds chicken wings, cut at the joint and
    rinsed in cold water
2 teaspoons salt
3 tablespoons evaporated brown cane sugar
Zest and juice of 4 limes
1 teaspoon acetic acid
4 ounces fresh mint leaves, minced
3 tablespoons minced green onions
¼ cup Cachaca (Brazilian liquor)

Preheat oven to 375 degrees.

In a large bowl, add the wings, salt, sugar, zest and juice, acid, mint, onions, and Cachaca. Toss to coat and marinate in refrigerator for 20 minutes.

Place wings on a wire rack on top of a baking sheet covered with foil and bake for 30 minutes. Preheat grill to medium high and finish wings until well charred. Apply lime glaze to charred wings. Serve with Confetti Salsa.

LIMEADE CAIPIRINHA GLAZE

Makes 1 cup

½ cup frozen limeade concentrate
¼ cup fresh lime juice
2 serrano chiles, minced
3 tablespoons minced mint leaves
½ teaspoon salt
2 tablespoons evaporated brown cane sugar
¼ cup Cachaca

Place all ingredients in a small saucepan and simmer for 5 minutes over medium heat; strain.

continued

CONFETTI SALSA

Makes 2 cups

1 yellow bell pepper, seeds removed,
 diced in ⅛-inch cubes
1 green bell pepper, seeds removed,
 diced in ⅛-inch cubes
2 orange bell peppers, seeds removed,
 diced in ⅛-inch cubes
4 Fresno chiles, seeds removed,
 diced in ⅛-inch cubes
1 habañero pepper, seeds removed,
 diced in 1/16-inch cubes
2 jalapeño peppers, seeds removed,
 diced in ⅛-inch cubes
1 teaspoon salt
2 tablespoons Melinda's Original Habañero
 Pepper Sauce XXX Hot

Place all ingredients together in a medium bowl and
mix to combine.

CAIPIRINHA COCKTAIL

Makes 1 serving

1 lime, cut in wedges
2 teaspoons evaporated cane sugar
1½ ounces Cachaca
6 ounces crushed ice
Fresh sugar cane
Limes for garnish

Muddle (mash) the lime and sugar in the bottom of
a mixing glass; add the Cachaca and ice and shake
until frozen. Serve in a highball glass garnished with
fresh cane sugar sticks and lime wedges.

Carnitas Chicken Wings

Fat has gotten a bad rap recently, but used in moderation it enormously enhances the flavor of anything it is cooked with. We take a cue from the local taquerias (taco stands) of Latin America and use some chicken fat to increase the flavor in these wings. Then we garnish with carrot escabeche to balance the richness of the wings. Allow 34 hours preparation time.

2 ½ *pounds chicken drumettes, rinsed in cold water*
2 *teaspoons salt*
⅓ *cup dried chile caribe (North of the Border Chile Co.)*
1 *tablespoon chipotle chile powder*
1 *onion, peeled and thinly sliced*
8 *cloves garlic, chopped*
4 *whole cloves, crushed*
2 ½ *teaspoons anise seeds*
2 *teaspoons ground canella*
2 *teaspoons oregano*
1 *bay leaf*
Zest and juice of 1 orange
2 *tablespoons brown sugar*
2 *cups chicken fat or duck fat*

In a large bowl, add the drumettes, salt, chile caribe, chile powder, onion, garlic, cloves, anise, canella, oregano, bay leaf, orange zest and juice, and sugar. Toss to coat and marinate in refrigerator for 2 hours.

Place the drumettes and chicken fat in a 6-quart slow cooker. Cover drumettes with parchment paper, place lid on cooker, and cook on low for 3 hours. Remove slow cooker insert and let the wings cool at room temperature for 4 hours; refrigerate for 24 hours.

Heat a large nonstick frying pan to medium low, and remove as much of the fat as possible from the drumettes. Fry on all sides, turning often. When the skin is golden, remove from the pan and serve with warm tortillas and Zanahorias Escabeche.

continued

ZANAHORIAS ESCABECHE

Makes 5 cups

12 ounces carrots, peeled and cut in coins
1 large yellow onion, sliced
2 red bell peppers, cut in strips
4 jalapeño peppers, sliced in rings
4 cloves garlic
3 bay leaves
1 teaspoon black peppercorns, slightly crushed
1 teaspoon dried oregano
1 teaspoon salt
2 cups white vinegar
1 cup water
2 tablespoons olive oil

Place all ingredients in a large saucepan, bring to a simmer, and let cook for 5 minutes. Remove from heat, cover with a lid, and let cool completely. Refrigerate overnight before serving.

Chicken Wing Tinga

Sweet, sour, savory, smokey, and spicy all describe what a tinga sauce tastes like. Chipotle chiles provide the spicy base and background, balsamic vinegar wakes up all of the ingredients with an acidic brightness, and the Mexican "trinity" of smokey peppers, onions, and poblano chiles rounds out this sauce from the town of Puebla. Try a variation of this recipe with thigh meat. When the meat is cooked, shred the chicken with the chiles and peppers to make tostadas garnished with Mexican crema. Allow 20 hours preparation time.

RED CHILE BRINE

4 cups water

3 tablespoons kosher salt

2 tablespoons sugar or honey

2 bay leaves

10 cloves garlic, skin on, crushed

1 tablespoon crushed black peppercorns

3 Fresno chiles, chopped

2 tablespoons dried red chile caribe
   (North of the Border Chile Co.)

1 sprig fresh rosemary

1 sprig fresh thyme

4 sprigs fresh parsley

Zest of 2 lemons

2½ pounds chicken drumettes,
   rinsed in cold water

Place all ingredients except chicken in a large saucepan. Bring to a boil, remove from heat, and let cool completely. Place drumettes and cooled brine in a large bowl and marinate in refrigerator for 12–18 hours.

TINGA

3 poblano peppers, roasted

2 red bell peppers, roasted

1 pound tomatoes, roasted

3 tablespoons olive oil, divided

2 small white onions, peeled and thinly sliced

2 cloves garlic

1 teaspoon minced thyme

8 chipotles en adobo, seeded and cut in strips

1 cup V8 Spicy Hot Vegetable Juice

⅛ cup balsamic vinegar

1 teaspoon salt

⅓ cup brown sugar

1 teaspoon pepper

Peel and remove seeds from roasted peppers, cut into strips, and set aside. Place roasted tomatoes in a blender, purée, and reserve.

continued

Remove drumettes from brine and dry on paper towels. In a large, deep frying pan, fry drumettes in batches of 3 using 1 tablespoon oil for each batch. Make sure to sear and brown each batch very well. When all the drumettes are cooked, remove to a warm plate and set aside.

In same frying pan, add the onion and garlic and sauté for 6 minutes until browned. Add the drumettes, thyme, pepper strips, tomato purée, chipotles, juice, vinegar, salt, sugar, and pepper. Let the sauce reduce, on low heat, for 45 minutes, or until a thick sauce is achieved. Serve drumettes with warm corn tortillas.

Yucatan Pibil Wings

Banana leaves are nature's perfect wrappers, which is why they are used in various cuisines around the world. They give off a sweet aroma and keep food beautifully moist as it is cooking. Cochinita pibil, pork cooked in banana leaves, is the inspiration for these wings, so feel free to substitute pork butt or chicken legs in this recipe. Banana leaves are also used as plates here, so the clean-up is a tropical breeze. Allow 2 hours preparation time.

PIBIL PASTE

Makes 3 cups

3 habañero chiles

1 pound 12 ounces Roma tomatoes

1¼ teaspoons cumin, toasted

1 tablespoon plus ½ teaspoon oregano, toasted

1¼ teaspoons allspice

1¼ teaspoons pepper

⅝ teaspoon ground clove

6 ounces achiote paste

3 tablespoons concentrated orange juice

Juice of 2 limes

2 teaspoons salt

¼ cup water

2 teaspoons Tabasco Chipotle Pepper Sauce

3 tablespoons apple cider vinegar

In a heavy-bottom cast iron pan, heated to medium low, roast the habañeros for 8–10 minutes; remove and reserve. Increase the heat to medium high and dry roast the tomatoes for 8–10 minutes. Place the tomatoes and habañeros in a blender along with the cumin, oregano, allspice, pepper, clove, achiote paste, juices, salt, water, Tabasco, and vinegar; purée until smooth.

PACKAGES

1 recipe Pibil Paste
2½ pounds chicken wings, cut at the joint,
rinsed in cold water, and pierced with a fork
2 medium onions, peeled and thinly sliced
¼ cup oil
6 banana leaves, cut into 12 x 18-inch pieces
and toasted over an open flame
5 banana peppers, cut in strips
2 tomatoes, sliced

Rub the paste on the chicken wings, place in a large bowl, and marinate in refrigerator for 2 hours.

In a medium frying pan, sauté onions in oil until golden. In the center of each banana leaf place 3 marinated wings. Top with 2 tablespoons of fried onion, 1 tablespoon banana peppers, and 1 slice of tomato. Fold the two sides of the banana leaf so they meet in the center and then fold the ends so they meet. Tie each bundle with a strip of banana leaf. Cook over charcoal embers, if possible, or on an indirect medium-low grill, for 40–50 minutes, or until internal temperature of 165–170 degrees is reached. Open the packages and finish charring the wings on the grill. Return to banana leaves and serve with Pickled Onions.

PICKLED ONIONS

Makes 2 cups

2 red onions, peeled and sliced
1 teaspoon pepper
1 teaspoon cumin seeds, toasted
2 teaspoons oregano
5 cloves garlic, halved
1 teaspoon salt
1 cup apple cider vinegar

In a large bowl, add the onions, pepper, cumin, oregano, garlic, and salt. In a small saucepan, heat the vinegar to a boil and pour over the onions; cover. Let cool and refrigerate overnight.

Cocoa Nib Chicken Wings

Salt-crust cooking is a centuries-old technique used to preserve freshness and moisture in foods. The crust also seals in and intensifies the flavors. In this recipe, I've incorporated cocoa powder into the dough and baked the wings inside a pie. You don't actually eat the pie crust, but it makes a dramatic presentation when you cut it open and find these delicious, moist wings inside. You can use sea salt alone or flavor it with your favorite herbs, spices, chiles, or anything else that sounds good to you. I've used chipotle powder to impart a rich, smokey flavor. This recipe is also great with duck legs.

SALT AND COCOA CRUST

1 pound flour, about 3 cups

8 ounces kosher salt, about 1 ¼ cups

2 tablespoons chipotle chile powder

½ cup cocoa powder

2 tablespoons pepper

1 cup egg whites, about 8

½ cup water

WINGS

2 ½ pounds chicken wings, cut at the joint and rinsed in cold water

2 tablespoons ancho chile powder

1 teaspoon chipotle powder or 2 teaspoons chipotle en adobo

1 tablespoon cocoa powder

1 tablespoon minced fresh thyme

1 tablespoon cocoa butter* or coconut oil

Preheat oven to 400 degrees.

Combine all the crust ingredients together in a large bowl, mixing well until a ball is formed. Add more water, a little bit at a time, if needed; make sure the dough is soft enough to roll out. Divide the dough in half.

Place wings in a large bowl and season with chile powder, chipotle powder, cocoa, and thyme. Toss to coat.

Roll half of the dough out to a 12 inch circle ¼ inch thick. Put the dough on a baking sheet that has been lined with parchment paper. Place the seasoned wings in the center of the dough in a single layer, making sure to leave a clean edge so that the top layer can be attached. Roll the top layer out to a 13 inch circle ¼ inch thick and place over the wings, pressing edges together to form a seal. Bake for 45 minutes.

continued

To remove the crust after it has baked, cut the edge with a knife and lift the lid in front of your guests. If you desire a crispy skin, place the wings and cocoa butter in a nonstick frying pan and sear for 2 minutes. Serve with Cherry Cocoa Nib Sauce.

*Cocoa butter can be found at Surfas Culinary District, www.culinarydistrict.com.

CHERRY COCOA NIB SAUCE

Makes 2½ cups

1 arbol chile
1 ounce ancho chile powder, or 3 whole
   ancho chiles, seeded, toasted
½ cup dried cherries
1 cup cherry juice
1 cup tequila or white rum
⅓ cup brown sugar
⅛ teaspoon allspice
3 tablespoons cocoa nibs, divided
2 cups cherries, pitted, cut in half
2 tablespoons brown sugar
¼ teaspoon smoked salt

In a heavy-bottom cast iron pan or comal, toast the arbol chile for 1 minute over medium heat. Place in a medium saucepan. Add chili powder, dried cherries, juice, tequila, sugar, allspice, and 2 tablespoons cocoa nibs; cook for 6 minutes over medium-high heat, or until liquid is reduced to 1 cup. Place in a blender, purée, and strain into a mixing bowl.

In a medium nonstick frying pan, add the pitted cherries, sugar, and salt; sauté for 2 minutes to let the juices release. Add the purée and simmer for 2 minutes, or until the sauce coats the back of a spoon. Add remaining cocoa nibs.

Olive Wings

The mix of olives in this recipe will keep your mouth excited for the next new taste and keep your mind challenged to try and identify which olive you just ate. I recommend a nice mix of Italian, French, or Spanish olives, but feel free to substitute your own favorites. Cracking the olives with the back of your knife will release their flavor even more. If you have the time, it's nice to remove the pits, but it's not a must. (Just warn your guests!) The addition of preserved lemon in this recipe brings a nice balance to the briny olive flavor. Martinis (always stirred, never shaken!) would be a fun accompanying drink for these wings.

2 ½ pounds chicken wings, cut at the joint and rinsed in cold water

1 teaspoon salt

1 tablespoon freshly ground black pepper

6 cloves garlic

¼ cup olive oil

12 Castelvetrano olives, cracked or pitted

6 green Cerignola olives, cracked or pitted

6 black Cerignola olives, cracked or pitted

6 green Catalan olives, cracked or pitted

12 Lucques olives, cracked or pitted

12 Picholine olives, cracked or pitted

6 Beldi olives, cracked or pitted

3 sprigs thyme, roughly chopped

2 bay leaves

2 cured lemons, pith removed and cut in strips

1 cup rosé or white wine

1 cup roasted Marcona almonds

Preheat the oven to 325 degrees.

Season the wings with salt and pepper and place into a turkey roasting bag with garlic, oil, olives, thyme, bay leaves, lemon rinds, and wine. Close the bag and place on a baking sheet. Bake for 35 minutes. Remove the bag and let cool for 30 minutes.

Increase the oven temperature to 400 degrees. Remove the wings and place them on a rack on top of a baking sheet lined with foil, and roast the wings for 10 minutes more. Place the olives and liquid from the bag in a small saucepan over medium heat and reduce sauce to half. Combine olives and sauce with wings after they come out of the oven and top with almonds. Serve with lots of toothpicks.

Garlic "Don't Even Think About Kissing Me" Wings

There are over 600 varieties of garlic. Forty cloves of garlic may not be enough for the garlic lovers, so let's look at some different ways to approach this recipe. Black garlic, the fermented Korean style, would be a good addition as it has a sweet and sour flavor and is perfect for a dip.

There are two subspecies of garlic, the soft neck and hard neck, found in the markets today. Popular varieties include the Polish, Italian, and German. Immigrants carried them to America in the 1900s. The hard neck, or white porcelain, with rather large bulbs is strong in flavor and spiciness. The artichoke, or white garlic, with the longer soft neck have a more generic taste and are a bit less intense. Allow 2 hours preparation time.

2½ pounds chicken drumettes, rinsed in
    cold water
2 teaspoons salt
2 teaspoons garlic powder
2 teaspoons pepper
2 tablespoons minced fresh rosemary
6 cloves garlic, mashed with 1 teaspoon salt
8 heads of garlic
¼ cup olive oil
½ cup white wine
3 lemons, cut in half

In a large mixing bowl, add the drumettes, salt, garlic powder, pepper, rosemary, and mashed garlic. Toss to coat and marinate in refrigerator for 2 hours.

Preheat oven to 325 degrees.

Cut the garlic heads in half and place in a large roasting pan with the marinated wings. Add the oil, wine, and lemons. Cook for 1 hour, stirring every 20 minutes. Remove pan from oven and remove the garlic cloves from the bulbs. Place the wings in a large nonstick frying pan and crisp the skin when you are ready to serve. Add the garlic cloves and lemons to the pan with the wings. If you like, garnish with some raw thin sliced garlic and fresh lemon juice. Serve with Easy Aioli and Charred Garlic Scapes Sour Cream.

continued

EASY AIOLI

Makes 1 cup

4 black or fresh cloves garlic, minced
½ teaspoon salt
2 teaspoons Dijon mustard
1 tablespoon lemon juice
1 cup mayonnaise

Place the garlic and salt in a small bowl and mash together to make a paste. Add the mustard, juice, and mayonnaise. Mix well.

CHARRED GARLIC SCAPES SOUR CREAM

Makes 2½ cups

1 bunch garlic scapes*, about 12, or substitute
  garlic chives or scallions
2 teaspoons dried chives
1 teaspoon smoked salt
½ cup Easy Aioli
2 cups sour cream
1 teaspoon pepper

Preheat a grill to medium high and grill the garlic scapes until well charred. When cooled, chop into small pieces and place in a medium bowl. In a spice mill, grind the dried chives and salt; add to the garlic. Add aioli, sour cream, and pepper. Mix well.

*Garlic scapes are the flowering stalks of hard neck garlic plants. The season for finding them is early spring.

Onion Crusted Wings

Certain cooking tools are indispensable and the Shyang-tian vegetable shredder is one of them, along with the Benriner Japanese Mandoline. These tools are inexpensive and I highly recommend them. Washington State produces the most onions in the United States, but look for local sweet varieties for this recipe. Allow 2 hours preparation time.

2 ½ pounds chicken drumettes,
    rinsed in cold water

2 teaspoons salt

1 large white onion, peeled and grated

3 tablespoons onion powder

1 teaspoon white pepper

3 large yellow onions, peeled

1 cup flour

2 tablespoons onion powder

1 teaspoon salt

1 teaspoon pepper

2 tablespoons dried thyme

In a large bowl, add the drumettes, salt, grated onion, onion powder, and white pepper. Toss to coat and marinate in refrigerator for 2 hours.

Preheat oven to 325 degrees.

Using a vegetable shredder, place the onions on the center of the machine and begin to cut shoelace strands. Grab a strand of onion and begin to wrap the drumette about 10 times around. This may seem like a lot, but the onion will shrink in the oven and fryer, so wrap as much as you can.

In a medium bowl, add the flour, onion powder, salt, pepper, and thyme. Mix well. Dredge each wrapped drumette in the flour and place on a baking sheet that has been lined with parchment paper. Bake for 35 minutes.

Preheat a deep fryer to 340 degrees with the recommended amount of oil for your machine. Finish the wings by deep frying for 2 minutes to crisp the onions and the skin. Serve with Onion Marmalade.

continued

ONION MARMALADE

Makes 2 cups

1 tablespoon olive oil
4 cups sliced sweet onions
½ cup water
⅓ cup balsamic vinegar
3 tablespoons brown sugar
1 tablespoon chopped fresh thyme
½ teaspoon salt, to taste
½ teaspoon pepper, to taste

Heat the oil in a large nonstick frying pan over medium heat. Add the onions and sauté until tender, about 10–15 minutes. Reduce the heat to just below medium, add the water, cover and cook until the onions turn a deep golden brown, about 50 minutes, stirring every 10 minutes for the first 30 minutes and every 5 minutes for the remaining time. (Add a bit more water if it starts to get too dry.) Add the vinegar, sugar, thyme, salt, and pepper and cook until most of the moisture is gone.

Pistachio Crusted Wings

Archaeologists have found evidence in Iraq that pistachio nuts were common food as early as 6,750 B.C. Its cultivation spread into the Mediterranean world by way of Iran from Syria. The pistachio grows well in southern New Mexico and is spiced with red or green chiles, our other important crops. These wings represent the colors of the state flag of New Mexico. Allow 24 hours preparation time.

CHIMAYO RED CHILE BRINE

4 cups water

2 tablespoons salt

3 tablespoons sugar

1 yellow onion, peeled and sliced

6 cloves garlic, crushed

*3 tablespoons New Mexico Chimayo
    hot chile powder*

1 ounce fresh oregano, chopped

*2½ pounds chicken wings, left whole
    and rinsed in cold water*

*1 cup red chile mustard
    (Old Pecos Foods brand)*

2 cups chopped red chile pistachios

In a medium saucepan, add the water, salt, sugar, onion, garlic, chile powder, and oregano. Bring to a simmer for 5 minutes, remove from heat, and let cool completely. In a large bowl, add the wings and brine and marinate in refrigerator for 24 hours.

Preheat oven to 375 degrees.

Place mustard in a large bowl; set aside. Remove wings from brine and dry on paper towels. Add the wings to the mustard; toss to coat. Place wings on a wire rack on top of a baking sheet that has been covered with foil. Bake for 10 minutes, reapply the mustard, and bake for 10 more minutes. Remove wings from oven and let cool slightly. Roll the wings in the pistachios to coat and bake for another 10 minutes. Serve with Orange Mescal Glaze.

continued

ORANGE MESCAL GLAZE

Makes 1½ cups

2 cups orange juice
½ cup orange juice concentrate
½ cup mescal or tequila
½ cup agave syrup
2 teaspoons coriander
Zest of 1 orange
¼ teaspoon saffron threads
1 habañero chile, cut in half

In a medium saucepan, add the orange juice, orange concentrate, mescal, agave, coriander, zest, saffron, and chile. Cook over medium heat and reduce to 1½ cups for about 20 minutes. Discard the chile, or chop and add back to the sauce if desired.

Squid Ink Wings or "Chicken of the Sea"

Squid ink provides a pungent, interesting flavor and intensifies the taste of whatever you are cooking. It has a salty earthiness similar to the taste of concentrated mushrooms or truffles. Squid ink and cuttlefish ink are used interchangeably, although cuttlefish ink is perceived as more velvety for pasta and rice dishes. You can buy it in prepared bottles so you don't have to juice a squid! In this recipe, the squid ink is incorporated into a tempura batter for the wings. The Lemon Mignonette provides a zesty dipping sauce.

2½ pounds chicken wings, cut at the joint
and rinsed in cold water

2 teaspoons sea salt

3 tablespoons red miso

2 tablespoons shitake mushroom powder*

1 teaspoon pepper

3 tablespoons squid or cuttlefish ink

In a large bowl, add the wings, salt, miso, mushroom powder, pepper, and squid ink. Marinate for 30 minutes in the refrigerator.

Preheat oven to 300 degrees.

Place wings in a turkey roasting bag and close, pushing out any excess air. Bake for 30 minutes. Remove wings from the oven and let cool slightly.

*To make shitake mushroom powder, place dried shitakes in a spice mill and grind to a fine powder.

SQUID INK TEMPURA BATTER

10 ounces pilsner–style beer

1 cup vodka

3 tablespoons squid or cuttlefish ink

1½ cups rice flour

1¾ cups flour

1 teaspoon salt

1 teaspoon sugar

Preheat a deep fryer to 375 degrees with the recommended amount of oil for your machine.

In a large bowl, add the beer, vodka, squid ink, flours, salt, and sugar; mix well. Dredge the wings in rice flour then dip in the batter and fry 6 pieces at a time for 5 minutes. Serve with the Lemon Mignonette. You could even throw some battered oysters or calamari in the fryer as well.

continued

Chef Heston Blumenthal, owner of the Fat Duck restaurant in England made this style of tempura batter famous. The use of vodka as the liquid in the batter doesn't create gluten when it comes in contact with the flour and burns off in the fryer so the batter is super crunchy.

LEMON MIGNONETTE

Makes 1 cup

3 tablespoons champagne vinegar
Juice of 1 lemon
1 tablespoon diced shallots
1 Persian cucumber
2 tablespoons diced cured lemon, pith removed
1 Fresno chile, seeds removed, finely diced
1 teaspoon finely sliced chives
⅜ teaspoon Fleur de sel (sea salt)
¼ teaspoon ground Tellicherry black pepper

In a small bowl, add the vinegar, lemon juice, and shallots. On a mandoline, cut the outer skin of the cucumber, slicing 2 layers. Turn the cucumber a quarter turn and make 2 more slices. Continue until you reach the starting point; you should end with a rectangle. Using as much green part as possible, dice 2 tablespoons and add to the shallots. Add the lemon, chile, chives, salt, and pepper. Mix well.

Resources

North of the Border Chile Company

P.O. Box 433

Tesuque, NM 87574

(505) 982.0681

(800) 860.0681

www.northoftheborder.net

New Mexican dried green chile powder and caribe flakes.

Kalustyan's

123 Lexington Ave.

New York, NY 10016

(212) 685.3451

(212) 683.8458, Fax

www.kalustyans.com

Assorted dried chiles, yogurt chiles, sun-dried chiles, Aleppo chile, dried spices, aji Amarillo, aji panca, and ghost chiles.

Los Chileros

P.O. Box 6215

Santa Fe, NM 87502

(888) EAT-CHILE

(505) 768.1100

(505) 242.7513, Fax

www.loschileros.com

Organic ancho chile powder, dried green Hatch chiles, Mexican oregano, chile caribe, chipotle chiles, New Mexican chile pods, and cascabel chiles.

Spanish Table

109 N. Guadalupe Street

Santa Fe, NM 87501

(505) 986.0243

www.spanishtable.com

Smoked, dulce, and bittersweet paprika, smoked salt, chorizo, Roland brand sun-dried tomatoes, anchovies, sherry vinegar, balsamic vinegar, saffron, pine nuts, Marcona almonds, Spanish olive oil, cuttlefish ink, and sun-dried garlic.

Bueno Foods

2001 4th Street SW

Albuquerque, NM 87102

(800) 952.4453

www.buenofoods.com

Fresh and frozen Hatch green chiles.

La Tienda

1325 Jamestown Road
Williamsburg, VA 23185
(800) 710.4304
www.tienda.com

Fresh Pimentos de Padron and Serrano ham.

Uwajimaya

600 5th Avenue South
Seattle, WA 98104
(206) 624.6248
(800) 889.1928
www.uwajimaya.com

Fresh Asian produce, soy sauces, and assorted Asian dry goods.

Amigo Foods

(800) 627.2544
www.amigofoods.com

Rocoto chile peppers, South American products, aji Amarillo chiles, green chile powder, and green chile caribe.

Surfas Culinary District

8777 W. Washington Blvd.
Culver City, CA 90232
(310) 559.4770
www.culinarydistrict.com

Fennel pollen, cocoa butter, and black garlic.

Anson Mills

1922 C Gervais Street
Columbia, SC 29201
(803) 467.4122
www.ansonmills.com

Polenta, grits, farro, and golden rice.

Metric Conversion Chart

Volume Measurements		Weight Measurements		Temperature Conversion	
U.S.	Metric	U.S.	Metric	Fahrenheit	Celsius
1 teaspoon	5 ml	½ ounce	15 g	250	120
1 tablespoon	15 ml	1 ounce	30 g	300	150
¼ cup	60 ml	3 ounces	90 g	325	160
⅓ cup	75 ml	4 ounces	115 g	350	180
½ cup	125 ml	8 ounces	225 g	375	190
⅔ cup	150 ml	12 ounces	350 g	400	200
¾ cup	175 ml	1 pound	450 g	425	220
1 cup	250 ml	2¼ pounds	1 kg	450	230

Index